DRIFTING UNDER THE MOON

First published in 2010 by
The Dedalus Press
13 Moyclare Road
Baldoyle
Dublin 13
Ireland

www.dedaluspress.com

Copyright © Ger Reidy, 2010

ISBN 978 1 906614 25 6

All rights reserved.
No part of this publication may be reproduced in any form or by any means without the prior permission of the publisher.

Dedalus Press titles are distributed in North America by
Syracuse University Press, Inc., 621 Skytop Road,
Suite 110, Syracuse, New York 13244,
and in the UK by
Central Books, 99 Wallis Road, London E9 5LN

Cover image copyright © Michael McLaughlin
www.michaelmclaughlinstudios.com

The Dedalus Press receives financial assistance from
The Arts Council / An Chomhairle Ealaíon

DRIFTING UNDER THE MOON

Ger Reidy

DEDALUS PRESS
DUBLIN, IRELAND

ACKNOWLEDGEMENTS

Acknowledgements are due to the editors of the following in which a number of these poems, or versions of them, originally appeared:

Poetry Ireland Review, Cyphers, The Sunday Tribune, The SHOp, Force Ten, Breaking the Skin, Present Tense (edited by Macdara Woods), *Foreign Literature* (Russia), *De Brakke Hund* (Belgium), as well as Mayo Anthologies and local press.

Thanks, too, to The Arts Council for the granting of a bursary in literature, to the Tyrone Guthrie Centre, Ian Wieczorek, Dermot Healy, Mayo County Council, The Heinrich Bxxxll Committee, Achill Island, The Linenhall Arts Centre, Castlebar, and Can Serrat International Arts Centre, among others.

For further details/information on the author, see www.gerreidy.com.

For Eleanor, Thomas and Deirdre

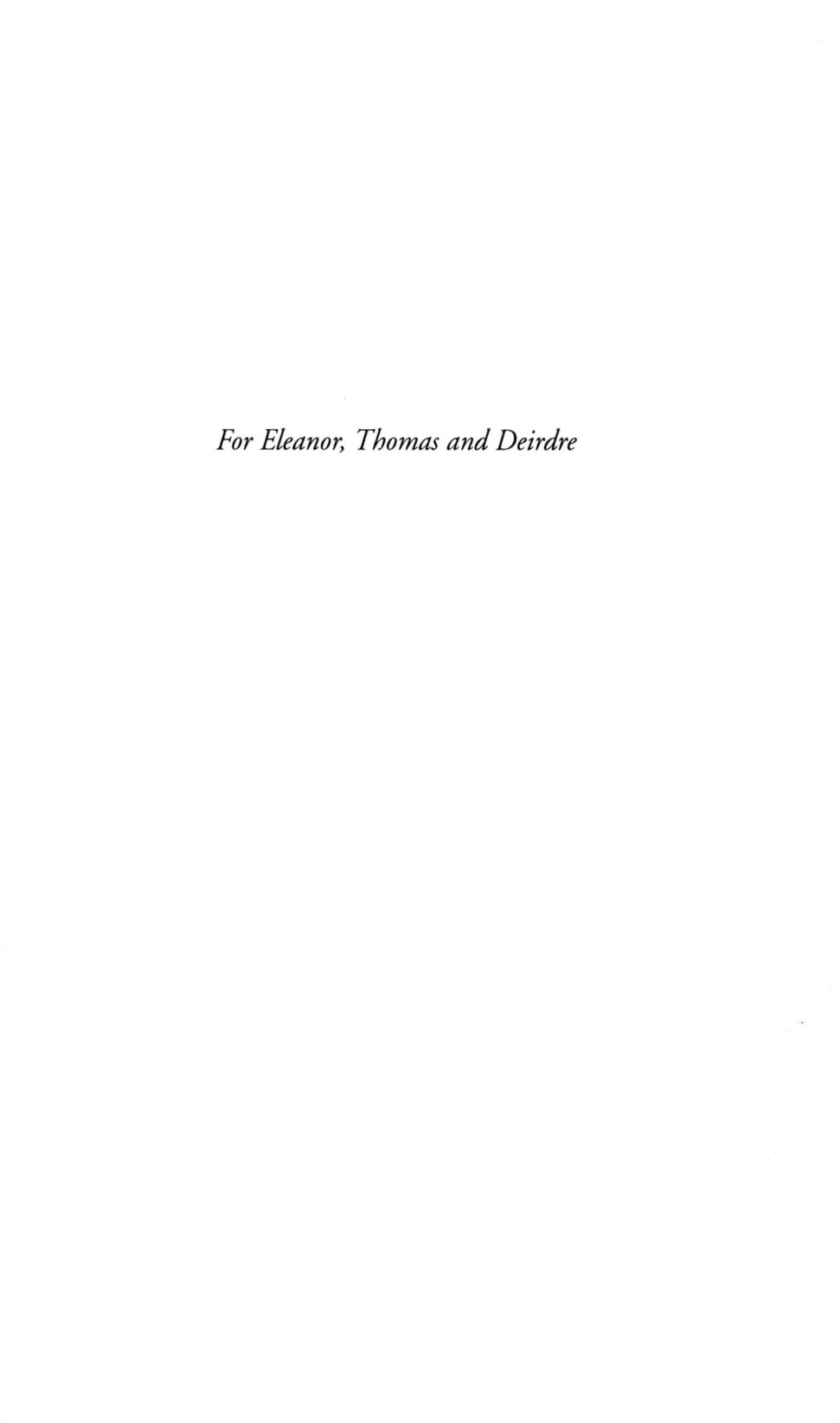

Contents

Relic / 9
The Pram / 10
The Reunion / 11
Dawn Transmission / 12
The Refinery / 13
Exiles / 14
Three Women and a Sunny Day / 15
Down at the Crossroads / 17
Piano Lesson / 19
The Decision / 20
Winter Evening / 21
Sunday Morning with Dog / 22
What My Husband Said / 23
Outside / 25
The Lesson / 26
Rocks / 27
The Scenic Route / 28
Fool's Gold / 29
Cows / 30
Shelter / 31
Pat's Game / 32
Returning / 33
The Musician / 34
Anniversary Photo / 35
Convent Girl / 36
Premonitions / 37
Dismantling / 38
Death in May / 39
Island Posture / 40
The Broken Mouth / 41
Afghanistan / 42
Waiting for Tar / 43
Midlife / 44
Questions / 45
Prayer / 46

Light / 47
The Chant / 48
Memory for the Day Room / 49
Ash Wednesday / 50
After Marina—for Eleanor / 51
Granny / 52
Spring Snow / 53
Among the Echoes / 54
Postcard for Claire / 55
Fencing / 56
Another Kind of Love / 57
The Escalator / 58
Snow / 59
Incident at a Station / 60
Saved / 61
Cumulus / 62
The Procession / 63
The Settlement / 64
Island Party / 65
Village / 66
The Wake / 67
Seduction / 68
The Room / 69
Lame Dogs / 70
It / 73
Flooding Near Leenane / 74
West / 75
The Absolutes / 76
Wilkommen, Roscommon / 77
After School / 78
Hindsight / 79
When to Say Nothing / 80
Initiation / 81
Cycling Home / 82
Another Spring / 84
The Silent Curragh / 85
Home / 86
Polonaise / 87
That Cloudbank / 88

Relic

When he parked that afternoon
in his own curious way,
how could he have known,
wading up from the meadows, fulfilled,
his wife and children around him,
driving back to the family homestead,
that it would never start again?

How could he have known
about the darkness waiting to greet him,
the minor chord that visited
after the second cup of tea?
All that remains now is the loyal Ford
disintegrating quietly beside a ruin,
facing downhill ready for the off.

The Pram

Every morning she wheeled it through the village,
into the butcher who never caught her eye,
around the priest who always did.
She wheeled it from town to town,
to the crowded beach in summertime.
On Sundays she took the top seat at Mass.
Nobody knew the mother
but everyone knows the father.

All agreed it was beautiful, empty,
but nobody said anything
because her flowers were perfect on the altar.
When her long hair turned grey
they took the pram from her.
She finally conceived in the hospital ward.
Nobody knew the mother
but everyone knows the father.

The Reunion

A single leaf falls from an elegant tree
laden with the sadness of a closed church.
It twirls, as leaves should,
and hesitates for a while.

When it finally arrives at the centre
of the dining room table
we realise this is an event
and there is nothing left to be said.

The silence developing
changes everything,
everybody departs alone
never to see each other again.

Dawn Transmission

Near the end,
when everything I lived for means nothing,
I might finally see what was always there,

a chosen poplar in a bog meadow
cymbaling like a tuning fork,
a change in the wind

gleaned by a shy hare
who waits to carry the news
into the next townland.

The Refinery

Skin me with a kiss from a cold corpse
lance me to the bone with a keen knife

immerse me in a bath of acid
clasp me in the vice of a country garage

stab me with the magic of an ordinary day
carve from me hunks of conditioning

beat me into a shape that will catch the wind
glean something useful from my essence

score me like the relief map of Connemara
distil me into alcohol drunk at my wake

abandon me at a crossroads in Roscommon
polish me finally into a shiny ball bearing

that drops from the mouth of a beautiful statue
onto a city square where a refugee sleeps

Exiles

Sometimes my little currach
lures me towards the edge
and my poor soul drifts into the depths.

Then the first bird clears his throat,
the school bus turns at the crossroads.
Forgiveness is a gift of seaweed

discovered at the front door.
Wonderfully lost we forsake home,
one to each table in the café

which is why we're all here,
exiled into memory,
slowly becoming what we must.

Three Women and a Sunny Day

We docked at the pier,
I held my wife's hands as we walked
up the windy path to the car park.
The July sun baked *The Sunday Times*
on the back seat of the Volvo. She said
we'd be in good time for the wine reception
at the Harbour Gallery, then mussels
and brown bread—our favourite—
planned for afterwards at the Wave Crest.
But she left her handbag on the boat.
"I'll be back in five minutes," I said—
then a fog came in, it wasn't forecast.

At the pier all was silent
except for some huge waves far off.
An old fisherman implored me to go home.
The sea crept over the pier.
In our boat, a young woman
wearing my wife's dress
listened to a Chopin polonaise.
She prepared a table for two,
caught my eye and laughed.
Then a great liner passed by,
the band playing 'In The Mood';
they all waved and knew my name.

It docked for a while, on board my father
was giddy in the throes of first love;
dressed up like a groom
he was waiting for someone.
The band stopped playing.

The captain greeted me with a glass of wine
and a terrible smile.
As the big engines groaned
I waved a silent goodbye
and ran back to the car where my mother,
impatient about missing the boat, scolded:
"We'll have to wait for the ten past eight now."

Down at the Crossroads

I refuse to drive her to Church
so Mother sets off walking
after she turns up the radio
to pump out Mass from Longford.

Across the street a naked bulb sways,
in the empty room over the butcher's shop.
From the chimney of a closed hotel
a Christmas reindeer swings in March.

A drunk is sucking stolen milk
on the steps of the derelict courthouse.
At the clock beside the Chinese,
a group of boys admires a Honda 50.

Ward's dog barks from the top of a coal-shed
while three women attend Benediction.
McHale scratches a *Winning Streak*
on the mudguard of a red tractor.

There's a bra and a pickaxe
in the front bucket of a JCB.
Mrs. Maguire is hanging out
the under-13s jerseys.

A doctor's daughter is playing Chopin.
A load of straw from Meath passes by.
On the radio an action-packed programme:
Sligo Rovers are playing Monaghan Town,

the players sheltering from a hail shower,
the game in injury time still scoreless.
The moon comes up over the meat factory.
A piebald horse is staring at his shadow.

Piano Lesson

Barely able to reach the switch,
a half-crown pressed into my fist
I raced up the stairs into your cosy flat.

All winter we battled with Strauss.
Why can't we do The Beatles? I protested.
Next week you played 'A Day in The Life'.

Middle-aged now, I hear it again
while I wait for the commuter train.
An old woman beside me gets up,

walks away with your lame step,
and I pursue her with a child's innocence
hoping that she'll never look back.

The Decision

He came home from the Manhattan Bar late,
parked the tractor under the bent sycamore.
She was waiting, listening for the ten paces
before the door opened, the dinner cremated.

They all looked up into his eyes,
the six children, the sheepdog.
He smiled as he finished his cigarette.
"I haven't time to beat you," he said. "It's eight,

if I start I'll miss the news at nine."
So he decided instead to wrap
his broad arms around them, holding them together
sheltered in a place they might never find again.

Winter Evening

All I know is that it was a long time ago:
mother in the garden, clothes drying on a bush,
pulling weeds from around the roses,
hands sprawled in a valium haze.

Father came home early from work, then silence.
As the frost descended, the sound of a showband
in the Temperance Hall came across the bog:
take me back to where the grass grows greenest.

Then time to feed silage to the shorthorns
in the limekiln field, to study the Punic Wars
and tie a shivering dog to a railway sleeper.
Father watched Hawaii Five-O.

The moon came up over the graveyard,
gleamed through their bedroom window,
and I watched as it caressed them both,
and dreamed of ancient battles.

Sunday Morning with Dog

In the first light my dog has chosen
to sit on top of the chair.
He barks at statues on the windowsill.

Suddenly every item here resonates.
Move the milk carton and all will be lost.
The hierarchy of characters awaits

an upturned fly to join them.
He is consigned to
the north-eastern corner of a blue tile.

Old men in county homes
and small boys trapped in cots
know about these things.

What My Husband Said

I fed the bull morning and evening,
checked him before bedtime.
Safe in his cosy shed all winter
he gaped out across the fields—
what more could I do?

One day he jumped over the gate.
The hail bounced off his back
as he ran around the perimeter
of the muddy field.
He looked ridiculous

ploughing up the wet soil
with his tail in the air.
After a week he walked,
still hoping to find a gap in the hedge;
he grazed on the short grass.

One morning I discovered
hoofmarks near the shed.
The rain was ceaseless
allowing floods to merge.
He plodded around the boundary,

his ears hanging down,
his ribs pushing through.
I left oats for him one evening
under a bush, he ate greedily.
One frosty night he climbed into the shed

and lay down in his old place.
I gave him hay just like before
but he couldn't look at me.
"Leave the gate open," my husband said,
then he won't break out.

Outside

I rapped on the great door
as soon as I was tall enough.
One year an old man answered.
I was not ready, so he banished me.
Winter nights left me wretched,
I could never go home
so I camped outside the wall.

One day it opened, a young girl came out.
"He wouldn't let me through for years,"
she laughed, "it's much warmer here."
So I passed through to another outside.
"You forgot this," the old man winked
and gave me a stone.
"That'll keep you warm."

The Lesson

I drove the cow from her dim stall
out into the winter every morning.
She stood beside the back door.
She could see a mud-churned field slowly
glazing over with hail beyond the dung pit,
but I never knew what she was looking at.

At midday she turned to face the door.
"Can I let the cow in now?" I pleaded.
"It's not dark yet," Mother decreed.
The cow listened for the sound of the bolt
and walked past me to her place.
We milked her and beat her out again.

When the knackers winched her
into a truck one hot day in August
her eyes were still searching for an answer.
Looking back I sometimes think
the cow was in love with my mother.
A lesson I would forget again and again.

Rocks

When we came home from the beach
my pet lamb was dead.
Father checked the others
and handed me the spade.

I pressed it into the bog water,
the bubbles breaking as I filled the clay
and fitted back the sod with hardly a trace.
"Did you put rocks over him?" he asked.

I never knew why he chose me until now,
on my knees, wrapping his things,
pressing him down away from me.
Once is enough to bury anything.

The Scenic Route

On Tuesdays I go all the way,
riding the cold blue line,
passing Civil War and Anarchy.
I stop at the red light for coffee
and watch the pink girl without the dog.
A lady I often meet says her grandfather
bought a ticket for Peace
on the far platform last century.
We laugh about that.
We pass through Aggression, Bitterness,
get off at Denial for lunch
and make eye contact at Commitment.
When we arrive at Anger
we change for Sadness.
So many stairs, the elevator broken,
when I reach the far platform
my varicose veins are killing me.
At the next stop we diverge.
I change for Therapy;
it's a faster route, I think.
Most get off at Family.
She goes direct to Shopping Central.
When I arrive in the evening
at the last stop—Oblivion—
I find her smoking a cigarette, looking
into the distance with a wry smile.
"You took the scenic route," she says.

Fool's Gold

You're in deep now,
the great door finally open
down at the black turf,
with only the faint echo of birds.

You can never go back.
The family gone,
you emerge with treasures
that are dismissed as fool's gold.

Below the water table
when the bank bursts
you'll be preserved
gnawing on all fours

at the bedrock,
waiting in vain
to be discovered, freeze-
framed into inarticulate verb.

Cows

I watched them scratch against a lone bush,
dejected on stony hillsides in winter,
or plod in single file through summer pastures
to gape over a warped gate,
heavy-eyed at milking time, gathering.
From them I'm learning stoic simplicity:

how to gaze across a lake at dawn,
how to doze in oblivious contentment,
how to forget a calf in a week,
and, when the time comes,
how to walk proudly into a mucky trailer
and swing with dignity from a hook.

Shelter

They taught the boys to chat about weather
when driving cattle into the German's garden,
how to smile and have cancer,
how to wait a decade or two
for the reward of a neighbour's death.

They taught the girls to dream of curtains
while drunken husbands make love,
how to bury five stillborns
outside the graveyard at night
and whistle a tune about Erin's Green Isle.

They taught me how to break bones
with a handshake and a smile
and grind them into powder
because the granite mountains that protect us
are made from the same dust.

Pat's Game

for Paul Durcan

We hopped the big leather ball
and waited for the return,
but it never came back;
the wind confined twenty-nine of us
under the same goalposts
despite switching sides at half time.

Father Pat kept reminding us
that we should all be defenders.
He didn't count own goals,
the final score was always nil:
nil, nil, nil—the dank weight
of a church bell at a country funeral.

One day late in the game
I was moved to full forward.
There was only a minute left.
She passed me the ball,
the goal was a mile wide.
"Just kick it towards goal," she said.

Ah, but then I remembered Father Pat,
turned round as the crowd roared,
kicked the ball right up the field
against the familiar wind
and scored in my own net.
I thought it wouldn't count.

Returning

I push open the door of your home place.
Cattle lie in winter beside a cold range
under the bike trapped in the rafters.

The bedroom stacked with hay and statues,
a swallow flutters against a high window.
I release it over empty haysheds.

You spoke of Butte and the Klondike
when I came here to buy eggs for mother
on the way home from the well.

I hurled myself against the walls of Mayo
until I could endure the peace of my own fields.
I pull out the door to trap the memory.

The Musician

The moonlight crept across your bedroom,
illuminating your toys one by one.
When it discovered the photo
of your dead grandmother
something knocked on the window.
You drew the curtain, but there was nothing.

You could not go back to sleep,
condemned to wander this world
carrying a guitar like a crucifix.
Years later your father said at some party,
"My mother was very musical, you know,
but she never had the chance."

Anniversary Photo

On the left, the girl who works in Motor Tax,
after she has left her kids to school,
her partner in charge of the vegetables
at the suburban branch of Supavalu.
Her sister changes bedpans
for country men who click their fingers,
the husband panelbeats second-hand cars
in a converted ballroom.
Padraig the builder has just bought a pub
and Monica turned the garage into a take-away.

Then there's Mum and Dad. She had
her left breast removed before the Alzheimer's,
and Dad was rationalised after thirty years
as part of a genuine improvement in customer care.

On the other side there's Angela and Michael.
She'd lost three before Peter was born—he's special—
while Michael milks the cows and drives the school bus.
Then there's John-Joe and Ellen,
the team who play country music after the bingo
and sing 'Nearer My God To Thee' at funerals.
And on the right, Seamus home from Australia
with his young wife Su Jong—
they hope to retire in the West.
For the camera they're all smiling.

Convent Girl

A thin breeze combs brittle leaves
from a lone mountain ash
near the pheasant dozing in the rushes.

A column of ridiculous sunlight
races down the hill to where she stands
at the crossroads, waiting.

Pythagoras and Yeats fill her head.
Shivering in her green uniform she sees
bogwater well up in the meadow.

When the School Bus scoops her up
the sunbeam, as it should,
moves on.

Premonitions

In a room where a nocturne was played,
in a railway café when the train has gone,

in a hayshed where a dog was tied,
in a country bar after a war,

in a bingo hall that sold raffle tickets,
in a ball alley where tinkers fought,

in a betting shop on a Saturday evening,
in the village square after a sheep fair,

under a bush beside a black cow,
beside a lake in a premonition of snow.

Dismantling

My father clutched the mangled steel
abandoned by his parents
and welded it into a similar shape.

With the remnants he carved
a shiny box for flowers
for us to plant.

On icy mornings we woke
to the shovel scraping the grate,
the saucepan banged on the table.

I listen to Satie with my children,
sleep late, picnic on the beach
and plant broad-leafed trees.

It's they who rap at my bedroom door
early on Sunday mornings
and slap dishes on the counter.

We defeat one sound with another,
terrorised that some generation
peace might break out.

Death in May

The whitethorn in reckless display,
winter's last protest confettied the crossroads,
McHale's tractor turns out of the sideroad
to feed the last bale of hay
to the sheep in the quarry field.

Appearing around the corner,
Eileen behind wearing your helmet,
you skid on a coincidence of leaves.
Beyond, an inexhaustible supply of girls
now silent in the Convent playground.

The lamb, curious, gazes across
at the wheel spinning to its perfect conclusion,
the eerie peace fractured
as we converge from all angles
to keep the traffic flowing.

Island Posture

He knows only wind and rain,
forever pointed into them
like a boat in a storm.

He suspects sheltered coves,
the twilight dapple of leeward shores,
moored yachts and restaurants.

Give him the blue honesty of hail
tearing at the shed roof
as the gulls bank in the gale,

the currach pulling a frayed rope
on a gathering swell
as he lands mackerel.

What he fears most is to find himself
becalmed in an alien world
where they honour him for the sacrifice made.

The Broken Mouth

As a child I left the playground,
crossed the river to an abandoned farm.

There I hid in a peaceful shed
where winter inmates had fled,

watched four gates at curious angles
and a thrush on a rusty mow bar

facing north towards the cow
in the churned mud, praising.

Somewhere near, the churches
must have been full of skulls.

I felt the silence after torture,
and looked up to see the clouds racing.

How was I to know that I could
never cross back?

Afghanistan

I brought him where he wanted to go—
past our space on the Fair Day,
his factory that's now a Youth Hostel,
under the bridge where he met my mother—
to the church where he lit every candle
and we sat in the front seat gaping
as they quenched one by one,
to his house where we beat the weeds down
to get to the front door.

All the time we talked
of the war in Afghanistan.
When we looked back we both knew,
this is how people get killed.
I tucked him into bed in the Home
and turned the light down.
He waved at me with a devilish smile, saying
it's terrible about the war in Afghanistan,
terrible altogether.

Waiting for Tar

When the black dog comes barking
I leave my bed and follow him
down the stairs and into the street.
I pursue him beyond the town limits
and into the black night
where he howls in the forest
as his echo fills the frozen valley—
as he clambers over the highest peaks,
as he plunges to the ocean floor,
while he discovers that the world is round.

In the morning, I chase him down
to Greevy's Wood where the sunshine
splashing between trees drenches the lane.
There he lies tamed beside
stoic labourers gazing into the distance,
standing together in silence
waiting for tar.

Midlife

Suddenly he woke to the sound of a bell
tolling beyond history.
The moon lapped at his bedroom window.
Outside the branches thrashed,
shadows soothing his naked form.

The room swam with ancestors.
At the window the curtains billowed.
Far off, a gleaming lake
in the pocket of a blue mountain.
Drifting now in life's open boat

he tore up the old rules.
That dawn they drifted down—
a snow flurry in suburbia,
absolution for his wasted life,
confetti on a new existence.

Questions

Where has he come from,
this man who lives alone
and has never left the parish?
Born in times of plenty or poverty,
he casts the same remote eye.
When the delegation knocks on his door,
before a great war or during a famine,
he knows the timeless answers
to questions they will never ask.

Prayer

Clare Island ran aground
at the entrance of Clew Bay
where sunlight tinselled the waves.

I am humbled into silence
at the fusion of river and sea.
Far off the squinting village streetlights

tell me that I must go home.
I bow my head and gaze at the stars
like an old bird drinking at the lake's edge

scanning the sky for a God to praise.

Light

I stood unsure on broken toys
and grabbed its first sunrays on a May morning,
ran to the top of our hill to gaze in awe
at the colour of cumulus towers over the bay.

On frosty nights I saw it reflect
off oily pools outside Marconi's chip shop,
spied it resting in cathedral pews mid-afternoon,
listened to the silence, absolving.

I felt the first terminal sadness after school
as it crawled up the floral wallpaper,
watched it trickle through the bicycle shed
over the pandemonium of old furniture—soothing.

I glimpsed lovers abandoned in moon meadows
as it angled its way towards me in a ruined cottage,
waited as it crept up a laddered stocking
while Michael Dillon announced cattle prices from Tuam.

But I never knew what it was until one evening
a watery sun peeked out between huge clouds,
and its last rays found the cracked bathroom window
and your naked profile, looking away.

The Chant

Hang old rags from a warped bush
and face east.
Sit on its gnarled roots till dawn,
listen to the ocean gales
tearing its boughs,
the hush of snow
arriving across a half moon.

Watch a fragile flower
emerge from the wet clay
with a stunted leaf
and a handful of berries
offered to the heavens
with raw hope of incarnation
in benign soil.

When the wind at last
comes off the mountain
you may hear in its branches
the chanting of ancestors
in a forgotten language,
beseeching that you accept
the fate of a simple tree.

Memory for the Day Room

Always have the strings tuned,
polish the chrome every day
so that when the sun, at some unique angle,
is reflected into her eyes
some year, now or in twenty,
she'll play a nocturne in the sacred room
and for a moment you'll waltz together beyond time.

Don't put a frame around it like a silly youth,
hang nothing on it, feed it with the full moon,
throw your house on the fire,
even yourself, to keep the flame alive.
Don't sleep—there is no time. Eat if you must.
Beg her to scratch her name on you before she leaves—
if you're lucky the infection will last a while.

A short life can glow down the road all memories go.
Let it be a two-fingered salute to the smiling matron
as you shuffle from a piss-reeking ward
when she rings the bell for medication
and they announce your birthday on local radio
as you nod forward and back
in the day room of their bright new century.

Ash Wednesday

A snow flurry swept up the valley
on a hard easterly, the low sun squinting.
I asked him how was the mother.
"She won't leave the room."
He shouldered a rope of hay
to the cows in the bog field.

As the light faded
he buried another sheep near the river.
He cycled down the mountain
to evening Mass,
brought home the ashes,
peeled the spuds in a plastic basin.

He looked out the window
at the dog tied in the hay shed
and knew that the seed
protected in the soul
would bring home the church bell
and the desperate absence.

After Marina

for Eleanor

She sells carrots at the railway station,
the lady who played the cello,
who survived the tyrants.
Today she sold three before she caught
the tram which wound its way
between gaunt tre,es to the suburbs,
to her room on the nineteenth floor.

The City Clerk has turned off the heating
so she huddles in the box bedroom,
reading Marina, listening to Dmitri,
keeping her pilot light glowing.
The blizzard whining through the cracked glass
translates into a metaphor
that forms a perfect quaver of snow.

Granny

She came home late, again,
and danced on the table with a man.
When they fell over she laughed,
burned a hole in the couch
before the grill went on.
Then, singing with Elvis,
the late movie
and the inevitable smoke alarm.
I had to turn up Wolfgang on my iPod
to drown her out, but The King won.
When I protested, she drummed
the broom handle on the ceiling,
shouting "Buddha,
when will they ever grow up?"

Spring Snow

Over the shoulder of a frozen hill
a curtain sweeping in from the north
muffled the sound of tied dogs barking.

The stars retreated south,
then one by one the trees bent,
heralding a wall of downy flakes.

Old cows stand in thaw water,
feeling the sun on their backs,
grateful in their own curious way.

Among the Echoes

He cycles into the village
past the old dispensary
and the abandoned school,
buys toffee and ice cream
and dumps his bicycle
beside the sheela-na-gig.
He wanders through the Abbey
and lies on a flat headstone
watching the woolpacks
despatched from Croagh Patrick.

He listens to the skylark
and the rasp of Gillespie's shovel.
Around him twittering crowds
gather for a wedding as he falls asleep.
Someone is dipping sheep in the ball alley.
The stream serenades midday silence.
He wakes to the shadow of the round tower
and the summons of a funeral bell.
Among the resonant echoes
Time's callous ratcheting continues.

Postcard for Claire

It happens like this:
when going back to work
where I must order steel for the bridge,
I turn a street corner

into a spring light that stabs me.
A freak tide blocks rush-hour traffic,
weeds flower and you are there
as a hard wind blows up the alley

where I must escape, deserted
except for the blind musician.

Fencing

As the pale light of a new year
announces itself on the shed gable,
you come to me
like the smell of burning whins
skirting over the hill from the half-parish,
or a signature tune from

some forgotten radio show
when I swapped marbles
and hid them in a limestone crack
and you whistled a Bing Crosby tune
as we receded into a Monet haze;
across a meadow, fencing, always fencing.

When you rested in the tall grass
you sent time into neutral.
One day on the hill we saw
a clothesline in September
filling with the first Atlantic wind.
We got up and walked in different directions.

Another Kind of Love

There is a noise in the dark,
the ashes being scraped from the grate,
dumped over the fence into oblivion,
then off to feed hay to gnarled cows in the shed.
He cooked rashers; we ate in silence
steeped in the pungent smell
of dung and turf smoke.

Some mornings I caught him looking away,
the way middle-aged men do,
then he smiled upon me
and told his favourite joke,
sang a dumb war-time song
he learned the year he met my mother,
and opened the yellowed curtains.

The Escalator

I must leave the beach now.
The bright light of the morning
yielded to afternoon haze
and the call of schoolchildren.
Like a failed hawker I gather my things.
A fisherman plods home dejected
with two mackerel in a plastic bag.

The first raindrops strike a distant hayshed.
Acrid smoke filters down
between the rushy drumlins
from Gillespie burning rotten straw.
The moon lays out its day's work
for the sea, but the weather distracts
like a woman on the opposite escalator.

Snow

A dog barks far off in a valley.
Outside on the children's swing
a lone blackbird knows.
The swans flew south yesterday.

The first flurry comes in over the woods.
On the far side of the river, everything is white,
I bathe in the flakes as they swirl.
Let in the winter, the oldest of friends.

When the time comes,
lay me on a cushion of half-understood words
and wrap me in the peace
that comes before snow falls.

Incident at a Station

We were waiting for the five-twenty.
Jim and I had planned to play
a mixed foursome at the club,
then dinner at Liz and Nigel's.

The sun was baking the window boxes
when an old train from the country pulled in.
A frail woman in black burst through the crowd,
flung herself at the engine, shouting

"This is how it was during the war,
I knew they'd come back for me."
But the doors never opened,
there was no driver.

The children laughed,
she was led away.
When the train moved on
darkness fell.

Saved

With acres of hay dry, he looked east
to see woolpacks sailing in.
Alone he gathered, but it was useless.
When he fell to his knees
they lumbered across the fields,
ran down the hills like Civil War heroes.

The storms waited in the next townland
until cartload after cartload
was pulled in by stoic horses,
until the shed was brimming.
He welcomed them, they ignored him.
Not a word spoken, they left.

At the crossroads they stopped.
When an old man waved
darkness marched across the border.
Such music on the roof all night,
peace knocked on the front door twice.
In the morning autumn lay abandoned on the doorstep.

Cumulus

for Brendan McWilliams

Abandoned at a crossroads without signs,
where blue mountains wait for rain,
and a truck collects milk churns,

I looked up but there was no-one,
only the distant echo of children
and woolpacks thundering inland.

Like a boy who absconds with a circus
I floated off with the clouds to faraway places
from which I can never return.

I smiled through the school window
when there was blood on the floor,
through the glass ceiling of middle age.

Oh, me and the clouds had work to do:
a hailstorm in a field of hay,
floods to block Main Street.

In the evening we died gracefully
on the edge of some Midland town
where giddy girls wait for the Dublin bus.

In winter we don't travel much,
but on warm June mornings
I'm up early waiting for the call.

The Procession

Collapsed on the bathroom floor
of a cheap hotel at dawn,
suddenly I hear a choir
before I see the mirage.

Wading across a meadow
from a previous century
they have finally come to retrieve me
with reassuring admonition.

They carry me back across the border
like a bold schoolboy
from a life spent, they might say, mitching.
Our voices retreating into a hazy afternoon.

They rap the old chant, alleluia, as if we were
on a tour bus coming home from Knock,
their habits swaying as we fade across a drumlin
out of view.

The Settlement

Even here, love happens,
in the twilight of slow decline
among the yellow seaside hills
reeking of winter sunshine
where a gnarled bush grows from a rock;

even here, where the broken cranes
nod to birds nesting in the wheelhouse,
where the guesthouse signs
creak in February wind,
where tired glory is sold on T-shirts;

even here, where cracked footpaths
yield to country weeds
beside the shrine to the drowned fishermen,
where after the first great hello
there were only whispered goodbyes.

But here too, a light comes on before dawn
like a crocus piercing through the snow,
and someone races through the night
because out here, like everywhere,
I have learned that this is all there is.

Island Party

When the little girl sang
of pain beyond her years
the wind gathered from nowhere
and howled through memory.

When the crucifix knocked
gently against the mirror
the widow emerged from the crowd
to politely close the door.

Village

A mongrel sleeps beside the petrol pump.
The local businessman double-parks.
The drunk, the whore, the beggar, the loner,
they're all here, but we know them too well.

A frail woman sweeps snow or sand
or weeds or needles from outside her front door.
A farmer drives by on a rusty tractor
pulling a trailer of hay or grapes, apples or maize.

A faded poster promotes trips
to Amritsar or Lourdes, Mecca or Knock.
Down by the dried river bed
beside a dumped refrigerator

kids smoke and drink and screw and talk.
An official perched in the Town Hall
has decided to change
the colour of parking tickets.

At the bus stop, two students
are sitting on the graveyard wall
looking in opposite directions,
waiting.

The Wake

This is where I found it:
after all these years escaping to cities,
probing deep into the night with friends,
when suddenly I was called home.

I took a shortcut with my father
under a half moon across the kesh.
We rested on a rock beside stunted birches
and listened to the fox in the next townland.

He told me stories of Civil War times
and the guns hid in the widow's house.
When we arrived, ushered into the kitchen,
our glasses full of whiskey,

we talked as if it wasn't there,
before it infected us with silence.
The corpse took our clothes off.
It didn't matter.

Seduction

One day she dragged me to sea.
Going home, nothing was the same,
I had flown out of the heavy soil.
I went back to the shore alone.

For months I asked the waves,
pleaded for an answer, but nothing.
Desolation that winter broke me,
washing back and forth, back and forth.

On a spring morning a boat came through the fog.
It stopped at the pier without a sound.
I knew nobody would be on board
and that I had to embark or be lost.

Behind me, wasted decades spent
trying to swim in the dry ocean;
before me a drowning, surely,
a welcome drowning.

The Room

When the wind rushed down the mountain
our house waited in the valley.
Watching the door in the forbidden room
one night I witnessed the opening.

A full moon beamed from the north.
Outside the gale threshed everything.
When a single violin played
my grandparents emerged in single file.

They picnicked in the front garden
and made plans for my children.
When they floated back into the room
I found my parents in the kitchen.

They were giddy like young lovers
as birds sang in the calm dawn
and dew glistened in the sunlight.
Years later when I climbed that mountain

I found the graveyard in a deserted village.
I sleep soundly now
knowing that they are in there,
whoever they are.

Lame Dogs

McHale sold a dry cow at the mart,
his wife died last year.

He has measured every woman here
but keeps his options open.

He leers at Mary from the barstool,
tells her that she was his first choice.

She laughs with a long wheeze
like a hearse with a puncture;

her pink knickers peek above her knee.
She occupies the world of support stockings

and discarded bingo sheets in community halls,
old phone bills pressed between faded china cups

and photographs of forgotten relatives
in USA Assorted biscuit tins.

After three gins, silence screams the truth
but they are rescued by the 3.30 from Doncaster.

Afternoon now, and the race is over,
and killing time a habit too ingrained.

Pretension hangs from him like the lining of a torn coat
and he must wander home in the cruel sunlight

past the bank manager's wife teasing a rose bush,
through the gangs of mocking convent girls

and the Pakistani street traders
with their cheap Knock virgins and music cassettes.

Gazing at the gleaming cabbage plants
he is shocked back to his father's garden.

He stumbles upstairs with a baby Power
to a room looking out on a railway track,

then falls onto the bed and watches
the billboard shadow creep across the room.

He is woken by the AA traffic report and the news
that Tony Cascarino has pulled a hamstring (again).

He stares vacantly out the back window
at the *Up Mayo* slogan on the handball alley,

at the girl next door sprawled on the lawn
and the boy in the other garden watching her.

A *News of the World* pinup looks down on him
but he decides to turn on the kettle.

He'll watch the farming programme on TV,
although he's long since sold his rushy fields,

and the silly English quiz show
featuring Larry and the two busty girls.

Then he'll wander into the Shamrock Bar
where the United crowd are singing karaoke.

Going home he peers at the racing results
in the bookie's shop beside the take-away,

stumbles down the centre of a moonlit road,
dropping chips into a cauldron of beer.

It

In the early years
when others spilled it fecklessly,
splashed it in the old man's face,
I observed its steady trickle
from the great lake,
but this too was futile.

Now the dam is open
as years turn into weeks.
Like water held in the hand I clutch it,
but, like love analysed, little remains,
only a crane surprised at a flooded river,
flying away into a wintry dawn.

Flooding Near Leenane

All summer the mountains were aloof,
the river turned away to the sea.
When the drought finally hit
the trickle was dammed.

The dry delta beseeched the hills
like some sheela-na-gig
but they could not meet.
Anxious to consummate,

the hills threw down rain
over the sodden parishes.
The flood swelled into the foothills
and John O'Malley's cow went under.

His wide-eyed daughter caught in a sunray
turned and looked up into me.
Recoiling, she recognised the answer—
"Can we go home now, Daddy?"

They walked down the road,
this carefree girl and the widower.
When she held his hand
the skies closed in.

The flood was rising around them both
but she couldn't get wet.
She knew about love
and how someone must go under.

West

The hotel leaning towards the pier
degenerates into a waiting room
suffused with tragedy and emigration
and portraits of Free State heroes.
Now *Sky News* and slot machines rule.

He stumbles west into oblivion,
bent against wind and hail.
Flung onto the islands
he looks out across the ocean.
Here only spray and gulls.

Behind him everything points away
in hope towards the mainland—
the huddled shacks around the harbour,
the warped bushes, the urgent stream—
It's night. He's armed with whisky and memories.

When they wheel him out
into a Victorian garden facing east,
the sun glinting over a calm marina,
before the old city glows, he rises.
Unable to straighten, he breaks.

The Absolutes

The last boat gone to the mainland,
we opt for that familiar voyage,
rowing to the smoky garden, oblivion.
The clock chimes, the wind howls,
you and I on the high seas,
music rocking the Delph,
before we sing out a desperate ballad,
arm-wrestling the absolutes into the dawn.

Wilkommen, Roscommon

One day you'll arrive here
at a wedding or a funeral,
poised under the benevolent shade
of clouds despatched from the mountain.
Its lanes are reclaimed by weeds.

Bypassed, with no river,
this inland town has no reason to exist.
Emigrants home for the summer
fill the hotel for a month,
the railway station now a museum.

September light soothes the vacant shops
as they recede into hibernation.
On Saturday night angry young men
from the country die huge deaths
in the manicured town square.

With girlfriends hoovered into the city,
their mothers water the flowers
under the *Wilkommen* sign.
For a moment I catch their fading beauty,
the saddest thing I've ever seen.

After School

She sat on the front porch
looking out across the winter garden.
Shadows danced on the wallpaper
as I ate three potatoes and a pork chop
while dreaming about Madagascar.

One day we heard the black wind.
It slid down the bare hill,
rushed beneath the tall pines
and licked at her ankles.
Doors slammed.

The memories ambushed,
she floated through the walls
dragging something terrible behind.
When the sunlight quenched the fire
around ten past four she went to bed.

Hindsight

My road has come to an end
at the edge of a great river,
its banks ornate with stunted sallies,
their cool shade caressing the shy trout.
The bog stretches to the horizon.

I'm shocked to see a cottage
on the far side occupied.
The woman in black is furtive
and disappears into a cart-house.
She sells eggs wrapped in newspaper.

In the next field an old cow
scratches against a low bush.
Her little gate swings perfectly
from a pillar buried in a fuchsia hedge.
There are wild hydrangeas in the garden.

I could wade across and greet her
but I would never return.
In the car mirror a young woman
walks naked across the water
but I can't turn back, I've already betrayed her.

When to Say Nothing

When I am robbed of the gifts
and all the fuss is over,
I will return to the place I knew
before I was interrupted,
where trails meet on a remote hillside
and the moon lurks under a lone bush,
to the company of someone
who knows when to say nothing.

Initiation

Swinging the pickaxe and sledge
he dug holes for himself,
ground everything into fine powder.
When he locked eyes, nobody survived.
He welcomed the blue knife of winter,
the barn door rattling was a lullaby.
He was a polished stone, an outlier.

Now in a hospital bed
he watches a spider swinging,
whistles an old love song at the nurse,
remembers forbidden dances in Lent,
and gazes at the town dump burning,
grateful for everybody and everything
including the view.

Cycling Home

It wasn't a bad night for March.
He'd freewheel all the way home from the pub
just in time to see the end of the match on TV.
The moon cut a triangle
into the wall of the derelict church,
anointed the wet roof of a distant factory.

A dog barked near the new graveyard,
frost clenched the priest's vacant house.
Cars from the village had passed
when the light was shrouded.
"Goodnight," she said with a low laugh,
and McGuire's Wood heaved in the gale.

He pedalled hard against the rain.
The first year he passed abandoned fires
at every crossroads,
and women driving ancient tractors.
Then he left the tar behind,
cycled on gravel roads with no fences.

He passed his parents saving turf.
A dog followed him on his birthday.
In summertime a mane of grass
played music on the spokes.
In winter, rushes whistled
when he slept under turf stacks.

He knew he was alive
when he cycled into a black donkey.
He ran after it, but it hid in low bushes.
That winter he heard her voice every night.

It stopped when he found the tortured animal
swinging from a mountain bridge.

He heard the sound of the ocean, twice.
When he cycled past a shrine, the light went out.
Coming through the village again,
the priest's house all lit up,
the church crowded, bicycles everywhere,
the haggards full, the graveyard gone.

When he saw his porch-light,
he heard the wind gathering.
As clouds throttled the moon
a car stopped, the door flung open.
"Hop in, it's raining," she said.
"I'm soaked already, I'll only drown the seat.

And anyway, what about the bike?"
"It'll be safe in McGuire's Wood," she said.
"It's downhill from here, but thanks anyway."
Moonlight drenched the bog meadows.
In the front garden a white horse grazed.
The match hadn't even started.

Another Spring

On afternoons like these
I am visited by the gentle death,
the mad new light filtering
through remaining wintry showers,
torn cloud wispy as your hair,
that light bestowed on our first meeting.

Now that I have accepted darkness
the sun detonates bushes on a low hill
like a glance from an old lover
at a country funeral.
What am I to do with another spring,
trapped in the inverted cage of love?

The Silent Curragh

The doorbell before dawn,
I wake from a dream—
the Titanic docked in the kitchen,
a glacier grew in the fireplace—
there's nobody there.
Two swans sleep in the purple sea.

Snow showers queue up over the bay,
the first breeze ruffles the birch.
As I drink coffee the storm rises.
Hailstones land in the fireplace.
My silent currach nudges the door,
waiting impatiently.

Home

Soot falls from your chimney
onto the cracked linoleum floor
and every morning the dog calls
to check the saucepan at the back door.

Neighbours bring you flowers
while their cattle graze in your fields.
You try to sleep beside a man
who's forever driving sheep up the hill.

Polonaise

Scar silence with faint music
from a sick childhood,

darkness with a silhouette
of a lost love,

isolation with the company of a woman
who lost peace.

Otherwise leave me dancing with all three
in the drawing room of middle age

tinged with absence,
culled from a pure memory,

bathed in a barely audible Polonaise
leaking from a closed room

on a wet summer evening,
prising the heart open.

That Cloudbank

The proud sheep on the highest rock,
the lark riveting the air with notes
and the bog water lapping in the breeze.
Sometimes a jet scraped the sky,
a fog tumbled down the hill,
or a fox came to drink in the moonlight.
Otherwise nothing, nobody.
I became part of this.

Skulls wash up at the lake's edge,
flocks of magpies swoop to scavenge,
winds buffet the dumb rocks.
Now I am exposed to seasons, old age,
and that bank of cloud coming in off the sea
that makes a normal man
call the dog, gather his jacket
and go to a place called home.